Tim and the Tiger

Written by Celia Warren

Illustrated by Bao Luu

Collins

Tim loved drawing tigers,
and developed his own style:
they were energetic, but scary,
with a very hungry smile.

2

Each tiger that Tim drew carefully
had a frightening facial expression,
with probing eyes of fearsome size
and a hint of real aggression!

Tim went with his sister Lucy
for a pleasurable walk.
Tim found a stone the size of his thumb
and discovered the stone was chalk.

4

"I know exactly what you'll draw,
I can tell by the look on your face,"
Lucy teased, as she glanced around,
"... once you find a tigerish place!"

But when Tim heard a chirpy song,
he changed his first decision.
He drew a scene of special birds,
with colour and precision.

Tim wrote the birds' names carefully:
flamingo, toucan and wren.
"Excellent!" said Lucy proudly.
"Let's try out the chalk again."

They soon found a new space for sketching,
magnificent, vast and flat!
Excited, Tim ran and began to draw.
"Not *another* stripy cat?"

This time Lucy knew she was right:
she watched in fascination
as Tim drew a muscly tiger with
no hint of hesitation.

Tim noticed the chalk was special.
Convinced, he continued to draw.
When Tim had completed the picture,
the tiger released a ROAR!

Lucy's expression was priceless!
Tim abandoned his piece of chalk.
"I think it's time," he whispered,
"to go on with our walk!"

Lucy grabbed the chalk from the ground.
She wrenched Tim's hand and they ran.
"Let's climb right up that giant tree
and make an emergency plan."

She clutched the chalk in her fingers,
concentration on her face.
"This piece of chalk could be the key,
to slowing the tiger's pace!"

She leapt down from their hiding place,
and sketched down on the ground.
Tim observed in fascination,
and chuckled at what he found!

The tiger watched intently,
preparing himself to pounce.
He sprang and landed on her ...
mattress, with a bounce!

The tiger landed gracefully,
"What fun!" it seemed to say.
The children had the impression
that now was the time to play.

Their first game was follow-my-leader:
the instructions were "Do as I do!"
The activity grew rather raucous,
a rip-roaring hullabaloo!

When the tiger suggested racing,
no one could match its pace.
Soon the others were on their knees,
aching, and red in the face.

18

But nothing can last forever –
destruction arrived with rain:
the chalky characters vanished,
their colours washed down the drain.

Tim frowned in deep frustration,
but Lucy retrieved the chalk.
"Think what inventions we might create
next time we embark on a walk!"

"We'll create a whole world of adventure,"
cried Tim, the chalk stowed in his pocket,
"from a chivalrous knight in armour
to a supersonic rocket."

Chalky drawings

 After reading

Letters and Sounds: Phases 5–6

Word count: 451

Focus phonemes: /c/ que, ch /sh/ ci, ssi, ti, ch /zh/ s /m/ mb /n/ kn /s/ c, ce, sc /r/ wr

Common exception words: of, to, the, said, do, were, one, once, our, their, whole, eye(s)

Curriculum links: Art and design

National Curriculum learning objectives: Reading/Word reading: read common exception words, noting unusual correspondences between spelling and sound and where these occur in the word; read words containing taught GPCs and –s, –es, –ing, –ed, –er and –est endings; Reading/comprehension: develop pleasure in reading, motivation to read, vocabulary and understanding by being encouraged to link what they read or hear to their own experiences; make inferences on the basis of what is being said and done

Developing fluency

- Your child may enjoy hearing you read the book.
- You could take turns to read a page. As this book is written in rhyming verse, model reading with lots of expression and emphasis on the rhyming words. Ask your child to do the same.

Phonic practice

- Your child is learning that consonant sounds can be written in different ways. Talk about this together. Focus on the /m/ sound in the following words:
  thumb   Tim   climb
- Ask your child to sound out and blend each word:
  th/u/mb   T/i/m   c/l/i/mb
- Talk about the different ways that the /m/ sound is spelt in these words. (*m, mb*)
- Now do the same with the /s/ sound: scene, decision, muscly, supersonic.

Extending vocabulary

- There are some very interesting words in this story. Turn to pages 2–3. Point out the word **frightening**.
  Ask your child:
  o Why do you think the author chose this word?
  o Do you think it was a good word to choose? Why?
  o Can you think of another word that she could have used instead of frightening? (*scary, terrifying, creepy*)